The Genealogy Do-Over Workbook

by Thomas MacEntee

The Genealogy Do-Over Workbook
Copyright © 2015 by Thomas MacEntee. Print edition.

Table of Contents

Introduction

Back in December 2014, I made a big announcement online and in social media: **Genealogy and I are parting ways. Done. Finished. Game over.**

Have you ever said to yourself, "That's it! I've had it and it just isn't worth it anymore!" Well, have you? Sort of like the character Howard Beale in the movie *Network* when he says, live on air, "I'm mad as hell and I'm not going to take it anymore!"

By the end of 2014, after more than 25 years of researching my own family history, that is how I felt.

My Past Genealogy Research Frustrates Me!

While many who read my post thought that I was leaving the genealogy community or closing down my genealogy business, I had to clarify what I meant by "leaving:" Starting in 2015, I planned on setting my 20+ years of genealogy research aside and starting over. From scratch.

Seriously. How many times have you thought about doing the same thing? Did you start your research the same way I did, by just collecting names, grabbing stuff from other online trees, or pasting text into your genealogy software? Lately, has the prospect of going back and citing sources or proving facts and evidence brought you down and ruined your genealogy buzz? Do you throw up your hands and say, "I give up!" only to return to the same review and edit process days or weeks later?

If you are like me, you need a genealogy makeover. Better yet, a Genealogy Do-Over. That is what I decided to call the journey upon which I embarked in early 2015. Now I want you to come along.

Genealogy Do-Over: A New Journey of Genealogical Discovery

Here is the short summary of The Genealogy Do-Over: I set aside everything* related to my genealogy research including notebooks, papers, and even digitized files and my genealogy database files and **START OVER**. I'm hitting the reset button. I'm allowing myself to have a do-over! (* certain items such as vital records ordered and paid for or research gathered on long-distance trips can be retained).

Since I started my initial research, much has changed in the areas of genealogy research methodology and education. I now realize the need to collect facts and track them properly, including the use of source citations. I now understand the process of analyzing evidence and proving facts to reach a conclusion. In essence, I know a lot more about the "process" of genealogical research and I want to put it to use.

This is not to say that I have not been following proven guidelines when it comes to finding family history. For my research clients (mostly pro bono), I actually employ all the methods advocated by many in the genealogy community. However, when it comes to my own research from years ago, I am not walking the walk . . . I have just been talking the talk.

It is not always easy to "walk backwards" and review every bit of information gathered over the years. Instead, I wanted to do more than re-walk a trodden path: I wanted to head out from the same starting point and see where the journey took me. I knew I would have access to better tools, better knowledge and be better equipped for each twist and turn. Now, I encourage you to join me on this journey.

The Genealogy Do-Over journey is constructed of 12 mileposts or journey markers that are laid out over one year. You can choose to pace yourself differently. You can even decide to drop some of the less important tasks and add your own. Do whatever it takes to ensure that you are on a firm footing to finding your ancestors.

A short synopsis of the route:

- Take inventory of what you have, box up the physical items and set them aside.
- Move all digital genealogy files into a HOLD folder.
- Gather tools to research.
- Set research goals.
- Start with your own knowledge and write it down.
- Start tracking research.
- Interview family members.
- And more!

And then, month by month, continue with research, add more skills and areas of focus including citing sources, tracking searches, building a research toolbox, creating an educational plan, researching offline as well as online, and more.

By the end of the year, hopefully you will have completed a review of a firm foundation in genealogy and family history research skill building. I realize that some focus areas may differ; anyone along for the journey has the freedom to add or remove content. This program has to work for you and should not be something that you dread each month or that you find you are working against.

You're Invited – You Get a Genealogy Do-Over Too

I created The Genealogy Do-Over as a collaborative community effort to re-examine the way in which each of us has personally pursued our genealogical research. My intent was to be honest with myself without beating myself up. I wanted to feel the joy of looking at one small fact and perhaps realizing that I never looked at it from all angles. I wanted the discipline of not following a possible lead just because it shakes or makes more noise than other leads.

Most of all, I wanted to be open to all possibilities on my journey of genealogical self-discovery and to enjoy that journey. This has meant researching genealogy with a plan, with a purpose, with sound practices and with the support of my fellow researchers. I do not intend to make this journey again. The Genealogy Do-Over is my chance, and your chance, to get it right!

How to Use The Genealogy Do-Over Workbook

The original premise of The Genealogy Do-Over, when it was launched in January 2015, was to create a review of topics with "how to" information each week at the GeneaBloggers.com site.

What was originally a one-time, 13-week cycle then grew to repeat over the course of three additional cycles. Throughout the course of the year, many participants commented that it would be convenient to have some type of workbook to collect all the materials and have them in one place.

So what is the best way to use this workbook? It really depends on your own genealogy work habits and your goals:

- Most readers will want to follow along month by month and tackle the topics as listed in the workbook.

- You are invited to "jump ahead" if you feel you have already accomplished the tasks involved with the current month's topics.

- Not all the topics are relevant for every reader, so feel free to create your own "do-over" experience using a selection of topics listed in the workbook.

- For those doing a "go over" – a review of existing genealogy research rather than starting from scratch – make sure you look for the To Do List for Review or "Go-Over" Participants at the end of each monthly topic section.

- In addition, do not forget the tutorial videos! The Genealogy Do-Over now has its own channel on YouTube at http://www.geneabloggers.com/gdovideos. New videos will be added each month to assist you with your Genealogy Do-Over experience.

* * *

I hope you get the most out of this workbook and feel free to send comments to me at hidefgen@gmail.com at any time.

A Genealogy Go-Over Instead of a Do-Over

Is the concept of "setting aside" years of genealogy research too much to handle? For some of the participants in The Genealogy Do-Over, it was not feasible to start over from scratch. Some felt comfortable doing a thorough review of their existing work using The Genealogy Do-Over topics as a guide. If this approach suits your style, then here is the best way to do a "Go-Over" instead of a "Do-Over:"

- Review each monthly topic and decide which topics will apply to your Go-Over.

- Pay particular attention to the To Do List for Review or "Go-Over" Participants at the end of each monthly topic section. These tasks have been created specifically for Go-Over participants based on the original Do-Over tasks.

- A simple way to do a Go-Over is to start with your own listing in your genealogy database software, and verify each data point such as birth date, marriage date etc. Can you prove each fact? Do you have a source citation for each fact? If so, then proceed to work on the information for your parents, then their parents etc.

- Develop a tracking system so you know which data points you have thoroughly reviewed and proved.

- Over time, you should improve your research, evidence evaluation, and source citation skills.

The Golden Rules of Genealogy

As you get ready for The Genealogy Do-Over, you might want to get a head start on the topic Setting Base Practices and Guidelines, one of the Month 2 topics.

I like the term "golden rules" because it invokes the spirit of The Golden Rule and focuses not just on my own research practices, but also on how I interact with other genealogists.

My Golden Rules of Genealogy

One technique that I use to come up with any list of practices is to look at them as recommendations: what key practices would I tell a new genealogist are necessary for success in tracing your roots?

A recent example is the 27 Golden Rules of Genealogy as put forth by Australian genealogist and blogger Alona Tester. Alona has sorted her list by Do's and Don'ts and she appears to cover many areas upon which most genealogists would agree.

Another example is a list that I put forth in my recent e-book 500 Best Genealogy & Family History Tips - 2015 Edition, entitled *Genealogy Rules to Live By*:

1. **There is No Easy Button in Genealogy.** You will work hard to find your ancestors. Genealogy will require more than passion; it will require skills, smarts and dedication. Do not believe the hype of instant hints, smart matches and shaky

leaves. If it were that easy, the journey of discovering our roots would have little or no meaning.

2. **Research from a Place of "I Don't Know."** Your genealogy research will likely run counter to your cherished family stories. It will upend your preconceived notions about certain events and people. It will change the way you think about your ancestors. This can only happen if you research with an open mind and take off the blinders.

3. **Track Your Work and Cite Your Sources.** When I started out in genealogy, I will admit I was a name collector and would "dump" almost any name into my database. Years later, I am crossing out entire branches of a tree that never really should have been "grafted" on to mine. Use a research log, track your work, cite your sources, and analyze data before it is entered into any software or online family tree program.

4. **Ask for Help.** The genealogy community is populated with people of all skill levels and areas of expertise, most of whom want to assist others. There are no stupid questions; we all started as beginners. There is no right way to ask. Post a query on Facebook, ask a question during a webinar, or email your favorite genealogy rock star.

5. **You Can't Edit a Blank Page.** Which means: you have to start in order to have something to work with. That project you keep putting off, like publishing your family history, will not complete itself. Commit yourself to move from "obsession" to "reality." Remember: *A year from now, you will wish you had started today*.

6. **Work and Think Like Your Ancestors.** While I am not sure about your ancestors, mine were resourceful and developed tools and skills to get what they wanted. They were not "educated" *per se*, but they had "street smarts" and knew where to go so they could learn new things. Also, make sure you have a plan; my ancestors did not just wake up one day and on a whim decide to come to America and make a better life. They had a plan, they had a network of people to help them, and they made it happen.

7. **You Do Not Own Your Ancestors.** Researching your roots can create emotional connections to not only your ancestors, but to the actual research itself. Many people become

"possessive" of their ancestors and fail to realize that a 3rd great-grandparent is likely the ancestor of hundreds of others. You cannot take your research or your ancestor with you when you die; take time to share your research and be open to differences in information and research when collaborating with others.

8. **Be Nice. The Genealogy Community is a Small Place.** While there are millions of people searching for ancestors, genealogists worldwide have developed a community with relatively few degrees of separation. Whether it is online in a Facebook group or in-person at genealogy conference, it is likely you will already know someone. Being "genealogy nice" is not fake; the connections with other researchers tend to be deep and genuine. We know that all of our roots are interlocked and a genealogist cannot always go it alone.

9. **Give and Be Abundant.** Exchange information freely with other researchers; do not hold data "close" to you or exchange it in lieu of something else. Most genealogists who have heard me speak know my own story of abundance: Do not let your hand keep a tight grip on information. Let it go. Once your hand is free, it can be open and ready to receive the next good thing coming your way.

What Are Your Golden Rules of Genealogy?

Are you ready to come up with your own list of Golden Rules? Since all advice is autobiographical (it is based on your own experience), look back at your past failures and successes and come up with your own list. When creating your list, you may want to divide it into sub-groups such as:

- Required
- Important
- Optional

Would you be willing to share them with others who are doing The Genealogy Do-Over in 2015? One option is to post them at your own genealogy blog or post them at The Genealogy Do-Over Group on Facebook.

Slow Down, You Move Too Fast!

When I first announced The Genealogy Do-Over over at my GeneaBloggers site in December 2014, many frustrated genealogists and family historians signed up for the "journey." In addition, as they joined The Genealogy Do-Over Facebook Group, the excitement became contagious. Nevertheless, in a short while, most people seemed "overwhelmed" and thanks to social media, that feeling can spread like wildfire! Here are some of the issues that were being raised:

- Some people were already worrying about whether or not they have to evaluate genealogy software choices and pick a new one.

- Others were concerned about how to name their files and how to organize their data.

- Still others wanted to know if they have to cite their sources or not.

Right now, your mind might be racing with many of these same thoughts and more. *These are all valid concerns*, but to be honest, they are a bit premature. Let's stop a minute, take a collective breath, and think . . .

How Many of Us Research: We Get Ahead of Ourselves

One of the concerns I had about posting the original Genealogy Do-Over topics too far in advance was exactly what seemed to happen: people either over-analyzed topics ("analysis paralysis") or simply skimmed over topics ("skimming"). This is exactly how I used to research.

I say "used to" because I developed The Genealogy Do-Over so I could share my insights into what has worked for me in the past. One of the major bad habits I had to break? **Getting ahead of myself and working too quickly!** Here is what I tweaked in my research habits and an area of focus over the course of The Genealogy Do-Over:

- **Capture everything and save for later**. This means using apps like Evernote to "clip and save" articles, links to new databases and even digitize documents and photos for closer inspection when time permits.

- **Build a good research toolbox and keep adding to it**. Use those capturing skills above, but add the art of "curating content" to create a set of resources that can greatly advance your genealogy research.

- **Create To-Do lists**. When I start researching a specific branch of my family, I always have a document open and available – a text file, a Word document, a spreadsheet or even a pen and paper – for writing down those nagging "I have to remember to do THIS" thoughts. Example: As I research my great-grandfather John Ralph Austin, I determine that his birth date means he would have been the right age for being drafted during World War I. So I enter on my to do list: "Locate World War I draft registration for John Ralph Austin." Get in the habit of *always* having a "catch basin" for these types of questions.

- **Pay no attention to that bright and shiny object**. Note how in the example above, I did not stop everything and look for that draft registration card right then and there. Why? There is an evil rabbit at the end of that rabbit hole where I think the draft registration card lives. Mr. Rabbit likes nothing better than to rob me of time and to distract me. If I do not place the task on a to-do list as it pops into my head, I will then go out in search of the draft registration card. And guess what? I find out that on the reverse it says "missing half of index finger on left hand" and then I go off trying to find out how he lost the finger and then . . . and then . . . And then it is 3:00 am and I have not accomplished ANY considerable research. And let's not talk about all my research goals I had for that night.

According to "fallible mom" and blogger Katy McKenna, "You can't make up with speed what you lack in direction" which applies to so many things including genealogy research.

The fact is that I did not even know I was working too fast and most of us do not realize it. I just happen to think it is one of the ways (or curses) of modern life. We might be working during one of Ancestry.com's freebie weekends and want to get the most out of that research time. Or we are working at the Family History Library and worry that we will not cross everything off our ambitious research checklist.

To be honest, what good is working quickly if it gets you where you are right now: *doing your research over for a second (or third, or fourth) time?*

Technology and Social Media to the Rescue

One of the benefits of The Genealogy Do-Over is that we have so many more tools via technology and the Internet than we did 30, 20 or even 10 years ago. We will be discussing tools such as Evernote, Pinterest and others throughout the workbook and showing you how they might be able to help slow down your research and keep you in the moment.

As a good example, I have set up a **Genealogy Do-Over Pinterest Board** (http://www.pinterest.com/geneabloggers/genealogy-do-overtm/) where I am collecting blog posts related to this project and resources that others are sharing over in the Facebook group. I personally use Pinterest to capture research goodies I want to remember and review later (this is a good use of Pinterest's Secret Boards function!).

Finally, if you are at your wits end trying to remember upcoming Genealogy Do-Over topics or a neat tool that someone posted on Facebook, there is help. I have created **The Genealogy Do-Over Mailing List** (http://www.geneabloggers.com/gendo-over-emails); sign up and each month you will receive a list of the new Genealogy Do-Over topics as well as a recap of resources and goodies shared during the previous month.

* * *

So as you prepare to start The Genealogy Do-Over, think about slowing down and putting the advice above into action. Create your own "to do list" for The Genealogy Do-Over. Start to collect resources. By doing so, you will get a head start on building good research habits and you will already be working smarter.

Remember . . . you have to make the moment last – that research moment. And get the most out of that moment. You may never pass that way again; you might not get a "do-over" again.

Genealogy Do-Over: The Value of a BSO

When you became interested in The Genealogy Do-Over, either as a participant or a "watcher," you likely saw a new term "BSO" mentioned by others. Is it a genealogy term? Is it an archaic cause of death? Is it a new technology? Not exactly...

The term BSO is shorthand for "Bright and Shiny Object" and can be anything from a shaky leaf on a genealogy website, to a newly found record, to a box of photos sent to you from a relative. If not handled properly, a BSO can cause your research to be derailed while you lose focus on your original research goal.

Genealogy is a minefield of BSOs, many of which can be avoided while others require action within a specific period. Here is how I handle BSOs in my genealogy research and why I believe conquering the BSO syndrome is the key to research success.

Your To-Do List – First Line Defense Against BSOs

I highly recommend the use of a To-Do List to track each "proof point" you are researching. A proof point is the fact you are trying to prove such as "Daniel OKEEFE was born in Ireland" or "Daniel OKEEFE married Catherine SULLIVAN."

A good To-Do List system will help you track various proof points, the records to use when researching, the date you started tracking a proof point and more.

Visit http://www.geneabloggers.com/okeefetodolist to download an Excel file example of a To-Do List for Daniel OKEEFE, my 3rd great-grandfather born in Ireland in 1828. As I used the 1860 US Federal Census to track information, I discovered he had a wife Catherine and a daughter Ellen. Those became new proof points in my To-Do List.

In addition, you are welcome to save this To-Do List format and use it as a basis for your own.

SHOULD You Follow that BSO? A Litmus Test

Discovering New Leads

Finding new leads is one of the keys to keeping us interested in our genealogy research. It makes sense, doesn't it? Even vendors like MyHeritage have capitalized on this "rush" of excitement we get when there is even the potential of finding a new ancestor. That is why we sign up for alerts such as Smart Matches or we click on a link that says "related record."

A new lead could come about simply from evaluating a record. A recent example: the World War 1 draft card for my great-grandfather John Ralph AUSTIN in 1917 lists that he had a wife and child. This was my first evidence of such information and my instinct was to stop everything and find out more.

There is a better way to handle these new leads:

- Use your To-Do List mentioned above and record each proof element to be researched based on the new information. Do this immediately so you do not forget.

- For the example above, one proof point entered would be "Determine name of wife of AUSTIN John Ralph" and another would be "Determine marriage date of AUSTIN John Ralph and UNKNOWN Wife of John Ralph AUSTIN."

- Enter the Start Date as the date you discovered the information and if you use a Notes field, briefly mention how you came about the information: "Based on World War I draft card for John Ralph AUSTIN reviewed on 14 April 2015."

Make it a habit to "capture" new leads each time. Not only will you begin building a list of research items, but also you will resist the temptation to follow that BSO!

Free Access Offers

Periodically, genealogy vendors will open up specific record sets to the public offering free access. Other times, for major events such as the end of the US Civil War, the vendor will offer specific records with specific access dates. Here is my strategy that I employ when there is a free access period for genealogy records:

- **Do I already have access to the records?** If it is part of a subscription I already pay for, I will not be attracted by the BSO. In fact, if I am a regular user, a free access period means the website could be slow and crawl during that period. Therefore, I make a note to come back <u>after</u> the free access period.

- **Can I get the records elsewhere?** Can I access them for free on FamilySearch or even Internet Archive? A BSO can become dull with just a little research as to available access points for those records.

- **Is it more cost and time-effective to hold off?** Let us face it, those records are not going anywhere. It is just the free access period that will expire. It might be a better use of my time to sign up for a special one-month subscription at the site when I have more time to fully dedicate my attention to the records. In addition, by then, I might have a whole slew of items to search in my To-Do List using those records.

One skill that I have had to develop over the years of doing genealogy research is how to best handle BSOs and make them work <u>for</u> me. Yes, it takes restraint. Yes, you can get "lost in the moment." Yes, it can be frustrating not to go off on that side journey. However, very few BSOs are so fleeting and ephemeral that they need to be followed right away.

Simply place the item in your To-Do List and follow the BSO when you have time and your mental focus is strong. Your genealogy research will thank you!

The Genealogy Do-Over – Month by Month

Month	Start	End	Topics
January	1-Jan	31-Jan	Setting Previous Research Aside Preparing to Research
February	1-Feb	29-Feb	Establishing Base Practices and Guidelines Setting Research Goals
March	1-Mar	31-Mar	Conducting Self Interview Conducting Family Interviews
April	1-Apr	30-Apr	Tracking Research Conducting Research
May	1-May	31-May	Citing Sources Building a Research Toolbox
June	1-Jun	30-Jun	Evaluating Evidence Reviewing Online Education Options
July	1-Jul	31-Jul	Reviewing Genealogy Database Software Digitizing Photos and Documents
August	1-Aug	31-Aug	Conducting Collateral Research Reviewing Offline Education Options
September	1-Sep	30-Sep	Conducting Cluster Research Organizing Research Materials – Documents and Photos
October	1-Oct	31-Oct	Reviewing DNA Testing Options Organizing Research Materials - Digital
November	1-Nov	30-Nov	Reviewing Social Media Options Building a Research Network; Reviewing Research Travel Options
December	1-Dec	31-Dec	Sharing Research Securing Research Data

Genealogy Do-Over – Month 1

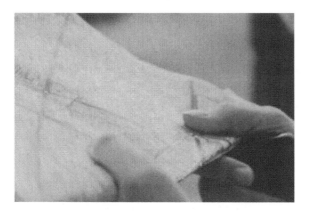

Month 1 Topics

- Setting Previous Research Aside
- Preparing to Research

Before we review the Month 1 topics, I want to provide a little pep talk since many participants may feel discouraged and overwhelmed. Remember: while The Genealogy Do-Over is a project-based learning initiative to improve genealogy research skills, **you should be having fun**. You should look forward to trying new approaches each month.

- **"When are we going to start research?"** has been a common question during The Genealogy Do-Over. Some participants wanted to dive right in and get online and look for stuff. My belief is that <u>we need to lay a firm foundation and take our time before we set out on our search</u>. A solid base of goals, procedure and tools will carry us through to the end and should not be improvised as we go along.

- **"There's too much information; I'm drowning!"** is also something I see posted on <u>The Genealogy Do-Over Facebook Group</u>. That is why you are here at The Genealogy Do-Over: **to gain skills to better manage the flood of data**. Keep in mind that Big Data is something we as genealogists will continue to deal with in the future and the amount of data increases each month and each year.

Learn to work smarter and determine the best data for your research.

Finally, remember that what I have put together for The Genealogy Do-Over is based on <u>my discoveries</u> in changing <u>my research habits</u> over the past year. ***Your mileage may vary***; which means that what works for me might not necessarily work for you. Feel free to make changes to the program by using different tools and different procedures. Just be true to your **Base Practices and Guidelines** (see Month 2 topics) and we will all likely arrive at the same destination: better genealogical research.

Setting Previous Research Aside

For many participants in The Genealogy Do-Over this can be the most difficult step in the entire journey: **breaking with previous research materials and with previous practices**. Remember that how you decide to "break up" with your research is your decision. Here are some guidelines:

- **Binders, folders and papers**: If it is not feasible to set them aside, you will need to be on your best behavior and resist the temptation to automatically consult these items.

- **Reserving specific items**: It makes no sense whatsoever to spend money (and waiting time) on records that you acquired previously. Make sure they are easily accessible and, when using them, you only refer to the actual data in the record . . . and do not look at any post it notes or notes you have written in the margins.

- **Digital holdings**: These files are the easiest to handle and move to a holding area, but at the same time their ease-of-access make them prime candidates for a "research crutch." Do not be tempted to go back to old research in these online files, if possible. Trust in the process and that starting from scratch and looking at records from a new perspective will bring success in your research.

Easy-peasy, right? More like "easier said than done" . . .

When I started doing my own genealogy research over again, I moved all my paper files into banker's boxes (a cardboard box used for document storage). I did hold on to several paper copies of vital records as well as some photos. In addition, I placed all digital files into a HOLD folder that, I am proud to say, I was not tempted to use!

Preparing to Research

It may sound odd for many of us to do "prep work" before researching. However, I found that if I took time to prepare my workspace and my mind for research, I had much better results.

For me, this means I will no longer research at 2:00 am if I am tired or half-asleep. It also means that I will no longer say to myself, "Oh I have 15 minutes before the roast in the oven is done, I'll look for Grandpa some more." One of my biggest problems in the past was **not starting or finishing the research process properly**. Moreover, the finish turned out to be just as important for me: with a good ending to a research session, I would know exactly where to pick up the next time I started.

So over the next month, **think about how you have researched in the past in terms of time, location, tools used, etc**. Consider making some changes. Write down some research "warm up" exercises and try them once we get to the research phase. Make a list of items that you must have available when you are researching (a copy of *Evidence Explained*, a spiral notebook, your copy of Evernote open on screen, etc.).

Month 1 To Do List – Full Do-Over Participants

- **Setting Previous Research Aside**: If you are sitting on a considerable amount of paper files and binders, try to sort through them and quickly pull those records that took considerable time, effort and money to order or collect. Another option is to simply put everything aside and then when you reach a point in your research where they are needed, place the task of locating that record on your To Do list. For digital files, try the same approach of moving them to a HOLD area. If you do not feel confident in your tech skills (and fear losing items or causing an error with your database software), simply commit yourself to not accessing these files unless absolutely necessary.

- **Preparing to Research**: Think about how you have researched in the past in terms of time, location, tools used, etc. Consider making some changes. Write down some research "warm up" exercises and try them once we get to the research phase. Make a list of items that you must have available when you are researching (a copy of *Evidence Explained*, a spiral notebook, your copy of Evernote open on screen, etc.)

Month 1 To Do List – Review or "Go-Over" Participants

- **Setting Previous Research Aside**: Work on organizing files, both digital and paper. Then locate essential documents that prove a relationship and either set them aside for future review or create an index . . . sort of like a Top 20 or Top 50 Document list.

- **Preparing to Research**: Make a list of you current research habits including when you research (time of day or week), the processes you use, etc. Review your list and determine if there are areas you would like to improve.

Genealogy Do-Over – Month 2

Month 2 Topics

- Establishing Base Practices and Guidelines
- Setting Research Goals

Establishing Base Practices and Guidelines

This topic offers lots of room for trying different approaches; however, most genealogists who have been researching for the past few years will likely have the same concerns and the same common practices.

I have already outlined many of my self-imposed guidelines in the **Golden Rules of Genealogy** chapter above. If I had to prioritize the areas and procedures, the list would include: 1) track all work, even dead ends, negative evidence and non-productive searches; 2) cite sources, even if in a rudimentary manner to note the "what, where and when" information about a record; 3) make the "first pass the only pass" which means slow down and spend as much time as needed on a document or source and wring every bit of information out of it. Later on in The Genealogy Do-Over process, I will have to decide on a file naming convention and a genealogy database software program.

Setting Research Goals

While I have listed this topic first in this month's series of topics, you really need some initial data (from the interviews above) before you can set research goals. Very often people set goals such as "trace my family's Irish roots" that are too broad or are based on family lore or assumptions.

Set goals based on information from initial interviews; do not worry if you believe some information is incorrect. Next month we will create research goals to prove or disprove data points. Create a simple list such as "verify birth location for _____" or "determine parents of _____." Next month these goals will form the start of your research plan.

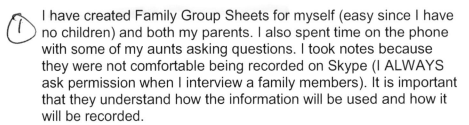

I have created Family Group Sheets for myself (easy since I have no children) and both my parents. I also spent time on the phone with some of my aunts asking questions. I took notes because they were not comfortable being recorded on Skype (I ALWAYS ask permission when I interview a family members). It is important that they understand how the information will be used and how it will be recorded.

Month 2 To Do List – Full Do-Over Participants

- **Establishing Base Practices and Guidelines**: <u>Do not gloss over this topic!</u> Spend some serious time outlining what procedures you will use to research, both online and offline. If a process is too cumbersome, you will not stick with it. Come up with a list of five (5) top procedures that you can handle during The Genealogy Do-Over.

- **Setting Research Goals**: Use paper, Evernote, OneNote, or any program to track your research goals.

Month 2 To Do List – Review or "Go-Over" Participants

- **Establishing Base Practices and Guidelines**: Review the procedures that other participants will be using; a good source is The Genealogy Do-Over resource page at http://www.bagtheweb.com/u/genealogydo-over. If you feel you already have solid research procedures, keep using them. If you need to change your research habits, write

down the changes and commit to them over the course of
The Genealogy Do-Over.

- **Setting Research Goals**: If you have existing lists of
  research goals, verify that they are in line with any family
  group sheet data. Create new goals based on new insights
  after reviewing the data.

②

③ Evernote to do list for E steel/Legacy

Genealogy Do-Over – Month 3

Month 3 Topics

- Conducting Self Interview
- Conducting Family Interviews

As we move into Month 3 of The Genealogy Do-Over, and since we have tackled the first few sets of topics, I want you to take yourself back to when you first became interested in genealogy and family history. Were you a teenager like me who watched the mini-series *Roots* on television? Did you have a family history-related assignment in high school or Sunday school? Or did you just hear others in your family discuss ancestors and you decided to do some research?

This month you are back at square one. **Back where you started**. However, you have more knowledge and access to more tools than that first time. In addition, you are going to heed the same advice you would give any other newcomer to genealogy: *start with yourself*.

Sit down and record what you know about your own history (birth, marriage, children, religious rites and sacraments, etc.). Then move on to your relatives. I realize that this time you are at a disadvantage: some or many of your relatives to whom you had access for information are now no longer here. Still, take time to do these interviews and you might be surprised at the results.

And once you have recorded information, you will set your initial research goals based on that information.

Conducting Self-Interview

There are many different formats to use for your personal interview including a simple written narrative, a bullet point list of dates and places, or a family group sheet. Make sure you take your time and record the important data related to:

- Birth
- Marriage(s) and Divorce(s)
- Religious events including bar/bat mitzvahs, baptisms, confirmations, etc.
- Children

An additional option is to actually write out your own mini-biography in your own "voice." You can then extract the data (next month) for your research log and you will have a nice memento to pass on to your family.

For my own Do-Over, I created both a personal interview and a family group sheet for my parents and myself. The interview is important; it is a "brain dump" of what I know in terms of dates, places etc.

Conducting Family Interviews

Once your interview is done, create a list of aunts, uncles, cousins and other relations who would have information about your parents, grandparents and other extended family members. Again, the format and method of interviewing is up to you. Some options:

- **Family Group Sheet**: If you have a fillable form (print or online) have your family members complete as much information as possible about their own immediate families.

- **Record an Interview**: With today's technology, it is easier than ever to record an interview. Consider using Skype and one of the several Skype recording programs. Alternatively, download an app for your iPhone or Android device. Yes, you will have to transcribe or record the information, but what can compare to preserving the voice of a family member as they describe their family's history?

Month 3 To Do List – Full Do-Over Participants

- **Conducting Self-Interview**: Select an interview format that works for you and enables you to extract the necessary information to launch your initial research next month.

- **Conducting Family Interviews**: Create a family group sheet for your parents and your siblings. One way to source these data points is to record an interview with each person and then complete the sheet, or have the interview subject complete the sheet and return it to you.

Month 3 To Do List – Review or "Go-Over" Participants

- **Conducting Self-Interview**: Consider conducting an interview of yourself based on your memories of important life events.

- **Conducting Family Interviews**: Review any copies of family group sheets in your files and check them for accuracy.

Genealogy Do-Over – Month 4

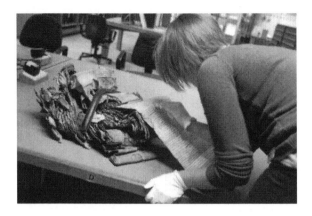

<u>Month 4 Topics</u>

- Tracking Research
- Conducting Research

With Month 4 of The Genealogy Do-Over, this is where, as genealogists, we "come home" to our favorite place: **research**. We get to actually take the information from our self-interviews and family group sheets and use it to find evidence to prove or disprove relationships and what I call "data points."

Do you remember returning home for the first time after a long absence, such as your first semester of college or on your first military leave? Things changed, didn't they? Maybe your mother converted your room into a sewing room or your father claimed it as his den or "man cave?" I hate to tell you this . . . but with The Genealogy Do-Over, coming back to research will never be the same. Now you will be asked to set up a **To Do List** (your research goals), track your research, and more. There will be data to enter, items to transcribe and eventually, thinking and analysis required!

This is how genealogy success is made. Most of you are part of The Genealogy Do-Over to change old research habits and to improve skills. What <u>was</u> is gone; long live the <u>new</u> research methods. And long live success!

Besides, haven't you heard that you can never go home again?

Tracking Research

One of the main issues I had with my OLD genealogy research method: I would not track data when I found it. I would simply enter it in my database, perhaps mark it as UNSOURCED and then tell myself I would clean it up later.

NO MORE! With The Genealogy Do-Over, the goal is to track your goals, what you want to prove and then – after collecting as much related evidence as possible – evaluate that evidence and prove a fact. Once proven, then it is entered into a genealogy database software program or an online tree. Solid information with solid source citations make for solid trees that don't fall over.

Genealogy Research Log

I have a genealogy research log that I use and that I recommend. It is a multi-sheet Excel file that can be imported into Google Drive as well as Numbers for Mac users. Past participants in The Genealogy Do-Over have stated that the file converts cleanly in many programs, even Open Office.

- **Excel Version – Genealogy Research Log**
  http://www.geneabloggers.com/genreslog

Some genealogists have asked if I could create a similar research log in another program such as Microsoft Word since some people find spreadsheets difficult to use. Due to the nature of tracking information and the need for a very wide table, Word just doesn't lend itself to a good genealogy research log format. Another option is to place all the fields in a "fillable form;" however, you would then have to create a new document for each record located. And then, how can you quickly see what you've found? Open and close a series of documents?

What you decide to use for a genealogy research log is up to you. If you've been opposed to using spreadsheets in the past, I just ask you to give the research log above a try.

Conducting Research

Once you have your research goals and a way to track them, then you are ready to research. This means both offline research at archives, libraries and repositories as well as online using various free and fee-based resources.

I continue to track down documents and evidence for each proof point on my To Do List. Right now the focus is on gathering the information, making sure I can remember where it came from and working on source citations and evidence evaluation at a later time.

Month 4 To Do List – Full Do-Over Participants

- **Tracking Research**: Review the research log above including all the worksheet tabs. Decide if you want to use this research log format or create your own. If using your own, include the fields you think are most important to track when doing genealogy research.

- **Conducting Research**: Using whatever tracking form you've selected, make sure you enter your research goals. Then start your research (with yourself and your birth date, birth location, etc.) and for each record found, make sure each one is entered and tracked. Copy a link to the record if it is online – you will want an easy way of returning to the record without having to do a search again. Make sure you extract as much information as possible from the record.

Month 4 To Do List – Review or "Go-Over" Participants

- **Tracking Research**: If you have never used a research log before, consider using the format above or creating your own. Another option is to see if your preferred genealogy database software has a way of tracking research; some have a To Do List option, others have something similar to a Research Log.

- **Conducting Research**: With your current research, start with yourself. Check to see that all information is accurate, based on your self interview, and make sure each point of data can be tied to at least one record. If something is missing a corresponding record – like a birth location –

then mark it as "unsourced" and add it to your To Do List for further research.

Genealogy Do-Over – Month 5

Month 5 Topics

- Citing Sources
- Building a Research Toolbox

Here we are in Month 5 of The Genealogy Do-Over and this month's focus is all about tools: finding and curating online tools to assist with your genealogy research <u>AND</u> understanding the basis of citing sources as a tool to document your research.

Building a Research Toolbox

For several years I've been advocating the following concept: every genealogist should create a consolidated research toolbox filled with various tools such as historical value of money calculators, links to historical newspaper sites, etc.

The reason? <u>Efficiency and increased productivity</u>. Think of how much time you spend looking for a link to a site you saved a week or a month ago? Wouldn't you rather spend that time looking for ancestors? On the other hand, when you need to calculate something – like how much $1 in 1910 would be worth in today's money, you spend time out on the Web searching for a site to do the calculation. Don't forget that each time you wander out to the Internet, you are at risk of being attracted by those BSOs ("bright and shiny objects") and time is wasted!

A genealogy research toolbox can take many forms: a blog, a website, an Excel spreadsheet or even a cleaned-up and organized list of bookmarks:

BONUS: Building a Research Toolbox video from RootsTech 2015

This past February, I was honored to present a live-streamed session entitled Building a Research Toolbox (you can watch the video below or visit https://rootstech.org/video/4053507280001 to view). In front of a full house of over 800 participants and with thousands watching live on the Internet, I explain the concept of a research toolbox and how it has helped my genealogy research. And visit http://www.geneabloggers.com/genrestools to download the *Building a Research Toolbox* syllabus for free!

BONUS: Tools to Get You Started

Here are some tools that I recently located while preparing for a recent online webinar. They are so useful that I can't see doing without them . . . so why not have them ready to access in a toolbox?

- **A Genealogist's Guide to Old Latin Terms & Abbreviations - GenealogyBank**
  http://blog.genealogybank.com/a-genealogists-guide-to-old-latin-terms-abbreviations.html

- **A Glossary of Archaic Medical Terms, Diseases and Causes of Death**
  http://www.archaicmedicalterms.com/

- **Abbreviations & Acronyms for Genealogy - The Accepted**
  http://www.geni.com/projects/Abbreviations-Acronyms-for-Genealogy-The-Accepted/3096

- **List of Occupation Abbreviations – GenealogyInTime Magazine**
  http://www.genealogyintime.com/dictionary/list-of-occupation-abbreviations-page-a.html

- **Spelling Substitution Tables for the United States and Canada – FamilySearch**
  https://familysearch.org/learn/wiki/en/Spelling_Substitution_Tables_for_the_United_States_and_Canada

- **Street Name Changes**
  http://stevemorse.org/census/changes.html

- **How to Use the Snipping Tool in Windows to Take Screenshots**
  http://www.howtogeek.com/207754/how-to-use-the-snipping-tool-in-windows-to-take-screenshots/

Citing Sources

True confession: Like many beginning genealogists, I did not always cite my sources during research. I was a name collector. I've evolved as my research skills improved and as I took advantage of educational resources. For me, citing sources is not about impressing other researchers or meeting any standards established by others. I cite sources so I can go back and find the original information. Plain and simple. Source citations are the equivalent of a trail of breadcrumbs along my genealogy journey.

So, why do we use source citations?

There are many reasons why a genealogist might want to cite sources while researching ancestors.

- **Establish Proof**. Cited material gives credibility to a fact or relationship while proving a connection.

- **Determine Reliability of Evidence**. Some sources are more reliable and make a stronger proof. Compare points of evidence based on their source.

- **Track Records and Resources**. Easily go back and locate records and their repositories. This is effective when the original record or a copy is lost.

- **Expand Research**. When encountering a difficult area of research, look for sources that were successful in making a proof and check them again for further information.

- **Discover Conflicts**. Locate contradictions in existing research or when new evidence is found.

- **Understand the Research Process**. When using another researcher's work, sources can give a glimpse at how that research was developed.

- **Placeholders**. Pick up a research project where you left off by looking at source citations.

How do I create a basic source citation?

A basic source citation has the following components:

Author, Title, Publisher, Locator

For the book *Evidence Explained*, here is a basic citation:

Mills, Elizabeth Shown. *Evidence Explained: Citing History Sources from Artifacts to Cyberspace*. Baltimore, Maryland: Genealogical Pub Co, 2007, p. 103.

- **Author:** Format can be "First Name Last Name" or "Last Name, First Name."

- **Title**: Format can be *Title* (italics) or Title (underline). In addition, article titles may precede publication title.

- **Publisher**: Format often includes publisher location, name and year published and sometimes appears in parentheses.

- **Locator**: Usually a page number or range of page numbers depending upon the source type.

In addition, for online sources you may need:

- **Accessed**: List date when source located as in "accessed on March 29, 2009" since online sites are known to disappear.

- **Examined**: List search criteria as in "examined for any reference to 'xyz'."

Following the Basic Source Citation format above, you will want to add more "locator" information when using records such as census pages, death certificates, etc. and also specify the name of the person(s) listed in the record.

> 1850 U.S. Federal Census, Lewis County, New York, population schedule, Leyden, p. 84, dwelling 1254, family 1282, line 36, Clarinda PARSONS, digital images, Ancestry (http://www.ancestry.com: accessed 16 October 2011); from National Archives microfilm publication M432, roll 523, image 168.

How can I access the citation format templates?

While I have added the source citation templates to the Genealogy Research Log (on the Citation Formats tab), visit http://www.geneabloggers.com/citeformats to access a list of common citation formats in a Microsoft Word document.

Month 5 To Do List – Full Do-Over Participants

- **Citing Sources**: If you own a copy of *Evidence Explained: Citing History Sources from Artifacts to Cyberspace* (either hard copy or digital), read Chapters 1 and 2. Doing so will help you understand how source citations are constructed and why they are so important to genealogy research.

- **Building a Research Toolbox**: If you don't already have a research toolbox, download and review the *Building a Genealogy Research Toolbox* handout here: http://www.geneabloggers.com/genrestools.

Month 5 To Do List – Review or "Go-Over" Participants

- **Citing Sources**: If you have cited sources for your previous research, review the cites and check them for formatting and accuracy. If you don't have a cheat sheet or template to help speed up the process, consider creating a way to use pre-set source citation templates.

- **Building a Research Toolbox**: Consider creating a research toolbox, especially if your current toolbox consists of tons of bookmarks or favorites that are not very well-organized.

Genealogy Do-Over – Month 6

Month 6 Topics

- Evaluating Evidence
- Reviewing Online Education Options

For Month 6 of The Genealogy Do-Over we turn to one the most important, and often neglected areas of genealogical research: **Evidence Evaluation**. As I've stated in the past, not determining whether a source was credible, would often come back to haunt me in later research. I've admitted this shortcoming and now I'm resolved to do something about it!

In addition, we begin to look at different types of educational opportunities available for genealogists. This month, the focus is on those offerings online, both free and fee-based. Ongoing education is a crucial part of not only becoming a good genealogist, but keeping your current skills finely honed and acquiring new skills!

Evaluating Evidence

Once I've gathered various bits of evidence for a proof point, such as my own birth date, and I've entered them in my research log, the next task: evaluating the evidence to determine whether my birth date can be proven or not.

In the past my evaluation of evidence consisted of saying to myself, "Well, if it is in a book it must be true!" or "If it is on someone's tree, why would they lie?" Then I would enter the data in my genealogy database program and go on my merry way.

Now, I'm using a process to really look at the evidence I've found and to "rank" it based on certain elements. The evaluation elements that I use are from an article entitled *Guidelines for Evaluating Genealogical Resources* by Linda Woodward Geiger. You can find this article, and many more, in the Skillbuilding section of the Board for Certification of Genealogists' website here.

I've included the basic evaluation information in a separate tab of my Genealogy Research Log so I can refer to it when evaluating a line entry in the research log. I also make notes in the Analysis column to support my theory as to proving or disproving my birth date.

Here's an example using a certified copy of my birth certificate that I have in my possession:

- **Source Type**: Derivative. It is a copy of the original record at the repository, in this case the New York State Department of Health, Vital Records. Some would argue that an official copy could still be called an Original instead of a Derivative, but for the standards I am using, I feel comfortable using Derivative.

- **Clarity**: Clear. I can read the text, it is typewritten or printed, and I don't need to guess at words.

- **Information**: Primary. Although this is a copy, the original birth certificate was filed soon after my birth and is very close in time to the birth event. It was also filed with an official government agency required to keep an accurate record of such events.

- **Evidence Type**: Direct. My birth date, location and other information is explicitly stated on the record; the information does not need to be inferred.

So, my birth certificate is "Derivative, Clear, Primary and Direct" as I call it. It would rank higher as a reliable record than say a birth announcement in the newspaper (not knowing who the informant was) or a Delayed Birth Certificate that is filed years later and based on one or more sworn affidavits by myself and/or others.

Finally, another valuable resource for learning more about evidence evaluation is QuickLesson 17: The Evidence Analysis Process Map at the Evidence Explained website.

Reviewing Online Education Options

Starting this month, The Genealogy Do-Over asks participants to starting reviewing options for genealogy education and the focus is online resources (we look for "offline" resources next month!).

As you can imagine, I'm a big proponent of not just genealogy education, but online genealogy education as well. Webinars are a big part of my own genealogy business and over the past five years, the genealogy industry has seen explosive growth in "distance education."

So why do we pursue genealogy education? Not only to become better genealogists, but also because new record sets come online or are available at repositories and we want to use them as efficiently as possible. In addition, we may discover an ancestor from a new location and we're not familiar with research in that area.

Here is a resource listing for free online genealogy education resources: RESOURCES Free Online Genealogy Educational Resources (opens in PDF). As you can see, there are some gaps especially in the area of Canadian, UK and Australian resources.

Month 6 To Do List – Full Do-Over Participants

- **Evaluating Evidence**: Consider following my example of implementing evidence evaluation into your genealogy research process. Yes, it can be time consuming, but just like citing sources, once you've gotten into the habit, it becomes easier and you feel more confident in completing the task.

- **Reviewing Online Education Options**: Review the RESOURCES Free Online Genealogy Educational Resources (opens in PDF) and consider creating an Education Plan. Start with small goals for 2016 and then look for webinars, videos and other online resources that can help you achieve those goals.

Month 6 To Do List – Review or "Go-Over" Participants

- **Evaluating Evidence**: If you are reviewing your existing research, it may be difficult to evaluate evidence if you haven't cited sources. In addition, some genealogy database software programs don't make it easy to evaluate evidence. Determine the best method for your current data; it may actually help to use a program such as Evidentia, Clooz or one of the other evidence evaluation software packages.

- **Reviewing Online Education Options**: There isn't much different for the "go-over" or "review" participants – we all need genealogy education whether we are doing a complete "do-over" or not. See the plans above and determine what is a good fit for your learning style and the gaps in your genealogy skills.

Genealogy Do-Over – Month 7

Month 7 Topics

- Reviewing Genealogy Database Software
- Digitizing Photos and Documents

Reviewing Genealogy Database Software

By now, many of The Genealogy Do-Over participants have been tracking their research and then evaluating the evidence to prove or disprove dates, names, relationships and more. The next step: enter proven data into a genealogy software program or on a genealogy website in order to share results and produce reports.

When I first started with genealogy, I purchased the latest version of Family Tree Maker from Banner Blue software (remember them?) and simply entered whatever I found (without evaluating evidence) into the program.

Then when I decided to pursue genealogy as a profession, in 2008, I opted to use a variety of programs, all at the same time. These included Legacy Family Tree, RootsMagic and Family Tree Maker. I also had my data in Ancestry.com on a public tree and on WikiTree. Why did I have my data in all these programs? Then, as now, I am often asked by vendors to beta test new versions and new features, so I had to keep my data in those programs.

Genealogy Database Programs – Are You Being Served?

I selected <u>Family Tree Builder</u> from MyHeritage since I have a MyHeritage subscription that I use and I like. MyHeritage is great for connecting with other European researchers and my German lines (Henneberg, Pressner, Herring) are where I need the most help.

I did a thorough review of available options and listed the features that were most important to me and my research. Every genealogist is different in terms of how they research so your choice should suit you and not work against you. Also, before moving to any new program, make sure you a) read the Terms of Services and b) understand how to import a GEDCOM file (that standard genealogy data file format. Some programs will not import notes, sources and other items. Make sure you don't lose data when moving to a new program!

Wikipedia has an up-to-date <u>Comparison of Genealogy Software</u> chart listing specifications. In addition, check out <u>GenSoftReviews</u> which includes actual reviews, many by genealogists and actual users of the programs.

Digitizing Photos and Documents

Understanding the correct way to scan and digitize your family photos as well as your research documents is an important part of genealogy. I can't stress this enough and I knew I had to include the topic in The Genealogy Do-Over.

Photo Digitization Best Practices

- Set your scanner to a high resolution, such as 300 or 600 dpi.
- Use the TIFF format and then copy TIFF files to create JPG or PNG files.
- Clean the scanner with a microfiber cleaning cloth. Remove dust, lint and fingerprints so you can achieve the clearest possible scans.
- Make sure the photo is in contact with the scanning surface or as close as possible to the surface; however,

often you can get a good scan right through a plastic sleeve, matt, or glass. Don't move the photo while scanning.

- Keep the photo lined up with the edges of the scanner to reduce editing later on.

- When transferring digital images to your computer, always save an original scan of the photo and then make copies of the file to be used for editing. Also, export to multiple file types.

- Use Photoshop Elements or your favorite graphic editing software to resize digital images for use with your favorite project.

- Remember to periodically backup your scans of photos and documents.

Photos: DIY or Use a Professional Service?

There are many different ways to handle digital preservation of family photos. You can take the DIY ("do it yourself") approach or use a service that will scan the images for you.

So what is the difference? The DIY approach may require you to purchase a scanner, learn the specifications and correct scanning settings, and then scan each photo. Once scanned, you'll need to rename the file, save it and then move on to the next one. The process can be time consuming to say the least. Using a service tends to be hassle free, usually guarantees a high-quality scan, but can be expensive if you have many items to scan.

If you decide to take the DIY approach, I highly recommend the book _How to Archive Family Photos_ by Denise Levenick. It has excellent advice on how to select a scanner as well as the best way to scan all types of photos. I also recommend Denise's handout from her RootsTech 2014 presentation, _How to Scan an Elephant: Digitize Your Family History from Artifact to Zombie._ Visit http://www.thefamilycurator.com/elephant/ for the free download.

One aspect of my current scanning regimen is the use of a wireless SD card by Eye-Fi in my Flip-Pal mobile scanner. I have the 8GB version, but I just noticed that Amazon is carrying the **Eye-Fi 16GB Pro X2 SDHC Class 10 Wireless Flash Memory Card** on sale for 30% off! Search Amazon for more info.

So why is having a wireless SD card so special? I can sit in my living room and through my wireless router, have the scanned image sent to my desktop computer or even to my Dropbox account. Also, many of the newer flatbed scanners have a slot to read SD memory cards!

If you decide to use a service, please take my advice: **review their services and make sure they are using the best equipment and providing you with the best high-resolution scan**. Many of the services, including superstores like Costco and Wal-Mart, outsource their scanning to vendors who are more focused on speed and quick turn-around rather than quality. Do you really want to take shortcuts with your family memories?

That's why I use Larsen Digital for my scanning needs: I've been extremely happy with the results. By using Larsen, I know I get expert results AND spend that scanning time researching my ancestors. Click http://www.geneabloggers.com/review-larsen-digital/ to learn more about Larsen Digital and to get a 15% off coupon on scanning services!

Documents: How to Convert Image Text to Searchable Text

The digitization of documents is different than photos due to this challenge: how do you convert the text in an image to text that you can search, copy and paste and use? The process employed to convert image text is called **OCR** or **Optical Character Recognition**.

Again, just like scanning photos, you can take the DIY approach or use a service. Keep in mind that the quality of the document will impact the OCR results. So if the document is old, faded and hard to read, the OCR process will certainly need review and correction. And, currently, handwriting OCR is basically unavailable.

If you have a flatbed scanner and it came with software, look to see if that software will OCR your scanned text documents.

Another option is to purchase a program such as **Adobe Acrobat Standard** that can quickly OCR scanned documents.

Alternatively, consider using a service for scanning documents; a good local option is your closest FedEx Office store.

Month 7 To Do List – Full Do-Over Participants

- **Reviewing Genealogy Database Software**: Review all the different genealogy database possibilities, including software that stores data locally, and online programs such as WikiTree. Select a program that meets all your needs including source citations, linking to scanned photos and documents, etc.

- **Digitizing Photos and Documents**: Spend some time reviewing how you want to scan your photos and documents. If you decide to take the DIY route, research scanners that work within your budget and technical expertise. And remember to thoroughly check out any scanning service you decide to use if you don't want to scan items yourself.

Month 7 To Do List – Review or "Go-Over" Participants

- **Reviewing Genealogy Database Software**: Also, decide if your current method of recording your genealogy research results are working for you instead of against you. If you decide to stick with your current system, make sure you've downloaded the latest upgrade and understand any new features.

- **Digitizing Photos and Documents**: There is no real difference in practices from the "All-In" participants; however, if you are sitting on digital scans of photos and documents you've done previously, review the quality and consider instituting the best practices listed above and "re do" those scans!

Genealogy Do-Over – Month 8

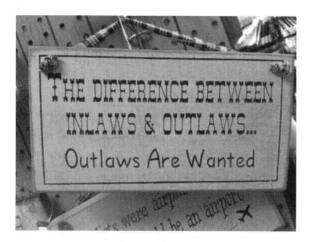

Month 8 Topics

- Conducting Collateral Research
- Reviewing Offline Education Options

Conducting Collateral Research

Many people confuse collateral research with cluster research or they tend to lump them together. For me, collateral research involves the collateral lines connected to your direct line ancestors. Most times this would mean focusing on the relatives of someone who married into the family – the wife or husband's parents, siblings etc. It also can mean distant cousins along your direct line. Also, don't forget those second and third marriages and step-children.

My definition of Collateral Research: A search for those who are not direct line ancestors, but who are considered part of the same family. These include siblings, half-siblings, in-laws and others through marriage. Example: take time to look at the siblings of a woman's husband or her husband's parents and who they married, as well as their children.

1. Start out with a direct line ancestor.

2. Spend time researching that person's spouse, including parents and siblings.

3. Record as much information as possible, no matter how insignificant it may seem. Include occupation, address and other details.

4. If needed, branch out with research on the siblings and other non-direct relatives.

Reviewing Offline Education Options

You have likely heard the term "not everything can be found online" when it comes to records and genealogy research. The same holds true for genealogy education. There are several large genealogy conferences as well as week-long intensives better known as "institutes" offering a chance to learn from nationally known educators and genealogists.

Over the past five years, several new institutes have popped up and I believe this will continue over the next few years in the genealogy field. Genealogists realize the value of working in a collaborative environment with other researchers and being able to network with others in person. There are some aspects of the institute concept that just can't be replicated online!

Review the list of large genealogy conferences and institutes in the United States and make plans to attend one or more in 2016 or 2017. Visit http://www.geneabloggers.com/offlinegenedUS for **Offline Genealogy Education – US**

Month 8 To Do List – Full Do-Over Participants

- **Conducting Collateral Research**: While some researchers prefer to work on an entire family as a "group," meaning parents and children, others "loop back" once they've work on all the parents and grandparents. No matter which approach you take, remember to utilize the research and evidence evaluation skills you've acquired over the past few weeks of The Genealogy Do-Over.

- **Reviewing Offline Education Options**: Review the list of available conference and institutes. Also, consider local genealogy conferences and attending local genealogy society meetings.

Month 8 To Do List – Review or "Go-Over" Participants

- **Conducting Collateral Research**: Those doing a "go-over" will want to review the children for each set of parents and look for missing children, other spouses, and verify all information such as birth dates, locations, marriages, etc.

- **Reviewing Offline Education Options**: Review the list of available conference and institutes. Also, consider local genealogy conferences and attending local genealogy society meetings.

Genealogy Do-Over – Month 9

Month 9 Topics

- Conducting Cluster Research
- Organizing Research Materials – Documents and Photos

Conducting Cluster Research

Last month we covered Collateral Research, which focused on siblings, in-laws and others considered to be within the same extended family. Cluster Research is different and is a large portion of the F.A.N. Club concept as put forth by Elizabeth Shown Mills (see QuickLesson 11: Identity Problems & the FAN Principle at the Evidence Explained website for an excellent overview of the concept).

Here is the definition of Cluster Research that I use for my own research: When you research the friends, associates and neighbors (aka F.A.N. club) who were part of the community of your direct line ancestors. Most times this means focusing on the geographical area where your ancestors lived or the locales from and to which they migrated.

Your Ancestors Had a Network

The saying "No man is an island," holds true when it comes to the daily lives of our ancestors and probably more so than daily life in the 21st century.

Understand that when a person or a family arrived in a new country, city or town it was likely that they already knew someone there. This may have been a relative or a friend of a relative. They may have been connected to the same hometown or same ethnic group in the Old Country. Our ancestors didn't just pick up and leave on a whim to settle down in a place that was unfamiliar.

When arriving in a strange place it was comforting to have some connection, something that was familiar be it language, religious belief or occupation. This made the transition easier and helped the person build a network upon which they could rely when needed.

Finally, if someone strange did arrive in a small town or even a city neighborhood, it was likely the townsfolk or neighbors wanted to know the following:

- Who were they?
- Where did they come from?
- Why were they here?
- What do they intend to do here?
- What are they bringing with them?
- What are they leaving behind?

In many places, in order for a town to survive, it was vital to find out this information and determine if this new person or family was a good fit.

Best Practices for Cluster and Collateral Searching

- **Always use a research log**. Make sure you enter your finds in a research log, no matter how insignificant they may seem at the time. Remember, you are looking for data that will indirectly provide clues to your direct lines.

- **Formulate theories . . . and write them down!** How often have you contemplated certain theories about your research, only to forget them later? Make sure there is a "Possible theories" or "Notes" section in your research log. You'll find it easier to recall those ideas later on if you enter them right away.

- **Spelling counts!** However, not in the way you expect it to . . . Make sure you are employing spelling variations when conducting each search. Surnames changed over time.

- **Stop relying on records that are indexed.** The indexing process is not perfect and if you rely solely on your ability to find information through a search, you can't conduct effective collateral or cluster searches.

- **Try swapping given and middle names.** For many different reasons, individuals may have used different names at different times in their life. Search based on both given and middle names and search using different orders.

- **Search by address.** You might be surprised at who lived at a particular address before or after your ancestor was there.

- **Leave no stone unturned.** Be dedicated in your search efforts to perform a "reasonably exhaustive search." If you don't, you're only shortchanging yourself.

- **Search without boundaries.** Make sure you are searching over that county or state line if an ancestor lived in an area close to a border.

Easy-peasy, right? Again, it takes practice and over time you'll remember all the little tricks of performing effective cluster searches.

Organizing Research Materials – Documents and Photos

Since we're on the "down slope" of The Genealogy Do-Over, it is likely that you've accumulated physical items in your research such as documents, vital record certificates, photos, etc.

While next month we will focus on how to keep digital items organized, let's talk about using folders, binders, filing cabinets and the like. First, I need to admit that I have a strong bias towards digital . . . to the point where I'd rather have a PDF or scan an item than have a paper version. Nevertheless, there are some items that are irreplaceable in their original form so organize we must!

Best Practices for Organizing Genealogy Items

Here are some guidelines I follow when organizing my paper materials:

- **Think preservation as well as access.** I try to focus on not just organizing items and making them easier to find, but also ensuring that they will endure. That means using sound archival practices such as the proper materials to store photos, negatives and other items. Check out the resources at **The Family Curator** (http://www.thefamilycurator.com/) by Denise Levenick offering great advice on the ins and outs of archiving and preserving items.

- **Select a system that works for you.** Don't employ an organization method that you won't stick with especially when it comes to maintenance. Review the various methods that other genealogists use and pick one that's right for your research habits OR select elements from several methods and create your own.

- **Schedule maintenance time.** Use a calendar (paper or online) and block out one or two hours a month to do nothing but tidy up your genealogy materials.

- **Do I really need that item?** A huge part of organizing for me is "curating" which means being selective in what to keep and what to discard. For old genealogy magazines, I just don't have the space anymore to store them. And, it is easier for me to search my computer for that article I need than to leaf through magazine issues. So I've scanned the articles that I want to keep and toss the original. Better yet, when I subscribe to a magazine, I opt for the digital version. For books, I can scan them and then donate them to my local genealogy or library.

Resources

Here are some resources that I recommend when anyone tells me they need to get their "genealogy cave" organized!

- **The Organized Genealogist**
  (http://www.theorganizedgenealogist.net/) is a group of over 26,000 genealogists on Facebook discussing ways to organize their genealogy materials. Lots of collaboration and discussion as well as people generously sharing their tips and resources.

- **Organize Your Family History**
  (http://organizeyourfamilyhistory.com/) is run by blogger Janine Adams and uses the byline "Stay focused and happy while exploring your roots." This site is filled with helpful information from a professional organizer who happens to also be an amateur genealogist.

- **Cyndi's List – Organizing**
  (http://www.cyndislist.com/organizing/) offers links on every conceivable sub-topic related to organizing your genealogy materials: bookmarks, supplies, gadgets, etc.

Ready to get organized? I realize that you can't simply organize all your genealogy material in a day, but with the knowledge and resources above, here's what you can do: create projects and tasks for your To Do List and tackle them little by little.

Month 9 To Do List – Full Do-Over Participants

- **Conducting Cluster Research**: Like me, you may not be ready for cluster research. However, if you do reach a stopping point, make sure you have the cluster research knowledge and materials handy to work through your ancestor's F.A.N. club connections!

- **Organizing Research Materials – Documents and Photos**: Think of getting organized as an investment: why would you spend years doing research if at some point you couldn't locate what you've discovered? Set aside those crucial one to two hours a month and commit to a plan to get organized.

Month 9 To Do List – Review or "Go-Over" Participants

- **Conducting Cluster Research**: It is very likely that you have some dead ends, road blocks or whatever you want to call them in your past research. Try taking one person for whom you can find no real information, and identify their F.A.N. club connections. Use clues from records such as census sheets to find their occupation, their native country, their native language etc. Start slow and small

- **Organizing Research Materials – Documents and Photos**: Organizing what you have can be a HUGE undertaking. Review the resources above and don't forget that there are professional organizers who can help!

Genealogy Do-Over – Month 10

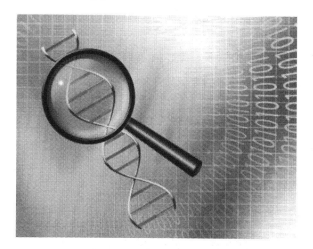

Month 10 Topics

- Reviewing DNA Testing Options
- Organizing Research Materials - Digital

Reviewing DNA Testing Options

One of my biggest research challenges has been to connect two different lines of ancestors: the MacEntees of Gardiner, Ulster County, New York with the more famous McEntees of Kingston, also in Ulster County. The only way I'll likely prove one of my long-held theories is through DNA testing.

Which DNA Test is Best? One Way to Start . . .

. . . is to read! That means studying various articles available online and in print. I've learned so much over the past five years from these great blogs that feature DNA and genealogy:

- **DNAeXplained – Genetic Genealogy**
  http://dna-explained.com/

- **Kitty Cooper's Blog**
  http://blog.kittycooper.com/

- **The Genetic Genealogist**
  http://www.thegeneticgenealogist.com/

- **The Legal Genealogists – DNA**
  http://www.legalgenealogist.com/blog/category/dna/
- **Your Genetic Genealogist**
  http://www.yourgeneticgenealogist.com/

DNA Genealogy Toolkit

Another great read – and FREE – is the Jump into Genetic Genealogy: Use Genealogical DNA Testing to Solve Family Mysteries e-book from Family Tree University. This guide will help you learn the terminology involved with DNA genealogy and you'll be able to differentiate between the various tests.

How about a wiki, like Wikipedia, but for DNA genealogy? That's what you'll find at the **ISOGG Wiki** (http://www.isogg.org/wiki/Wiki_Welcome_Page) created and maintained by the **International Society of Genetic Genealogy**. This site makes it easy to search for terminology, DNA test vendors, and more.

Interpreting DNA Testing Results

One tool I need to use more is **GedMatch** (http://v2.gedmatch.com/) which allows you to upload your testing results from various tests and run reports as well as connect with other genealogists using DNA testing.

Organizing Research Materials – Digital

While computers and the Internet have been a boon to genealogy researchers, with more data come more headaches including how to keep it all organized!

Danger Ahead: The Digital Dark Ages

Which of these two items do you think is more in peril of being lost: An original photograph from 1950 OR a digital scan of that same photograph? While the printed version might be lost, or consumed in a fire or damaged in a flood, consider all these calamities that could befall your digital version:

- Hard drive failure

- Accidental deletion of file

- Conversion from high-res TIFF file format to lower-res JPG format

- File corruption

- File format becomes obsolete

- Storage on outdated media such as floppy disks

- Over-correction of color and features using photo editing software

The truth is that there is no guarantee that TIFF or other file formats will even be around in 20 years. I'm sure that even with glasses, my eyes will always be able to see that 1950 photo! See *Google's Vint Cerf warns of 'digital Dark Age'* for an overview of this pressing issue.

Pick a File Naming Convention and Stick With It!

There are many different ways to name your digital files used in genealogy research. Some prefer a numbering scheme while others begin with the surname. What about married female ancestors? (I ALWAYS use the surname with which they were born . .)

My method right now, and one that works for me is as follows: **SLATTERY John Vincent b1888 WWI Draft Reg Card** tells me, at first glance, that the file is a World War I draft registration card for John Vincent Slattery who was born in 1888. I add the "b _____" segment since I have many ancestors with the same name, such as John Austin.

This method is loosely based on one developed by a current Genealogy Do-Over participant, Diana Ritchie. Visit https://www.facebook.com/groups/genealogydoover/permalink/52 8502823959046/ to read Diana's original post in The Genealogy Do-Over Group on Facebook outlining her file naming convention.

Metadata Is Your Friend

What is metadata? It is "data about data" but there is an easier way to get genealogists interested. What if I told you that there was a way for you to add information about a digital image to the file – such as the subject, data, location and even a source citation – to the file so that it is always part of the file structure? That is what metadata can do.

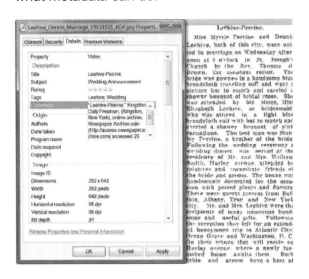

In the example above, I have entered my own text in the Title and Subject fields, added Tags and also placed my source citation in the Comments field (which holds 9,999 characters!)

You may not realize that metadata is already added to many of your digital files, especially when they are created. One example is a photo created with a digital camera or a smartphone. If you examine the metadata it will tell you the type of camera used to create the file, the file creation date, the resolution and sometimes even the GPS location of the photo.

So what about files that you've created, can you add and edit that metadata? Sure you can. An easier way to explain it is to watch a video recording of a webinar I presented called *Metadata for Digital Images*.

Visit http://flip-pal.com/videos/webinars/metadata/ to view.

Once you've mastered the metadata concepts, consider adding important metadata to each of your genealogy research files!

Organize AND Backup Digital Materials

What good is spending hours organizing digital files if you don't ensure their future accessibility? Every genealogist should have a data backup plan and also perform backups on a regular basis.

Try employing the **3-2-1 Rule**:

- **3 copies of each file**. This means one primary copy, likely your hard drive, and then two other copies such as in the cloud and on an external hard drive.

- **2 different media formats**. Don't store all copies on different hard drives or in different cloud platforms. Use different media such as hard drive, cloud, USB flash drive etc.

- **1 offsite copy**. This means do not copy files to a USB drive that you keep near your computer. Place it in a fire safe. Better yet, make sure one of your file copies is in the cloud which means it is not physically stored near the hard drive version.

Don't forget that backing up on a regular schedule is important as well. In the genealogy community, the 1st day of each month is promoted as **Data Backup Day** and is a reminder to all genealogists to future proof their research data!

Month 10 To Do List – Full Do-Over Participants

- **New to DNA Genealogy**: If you have not yet spent time learning about DNA genealogy, use some of the resources listed above and familiarize yourself with the various tests and terminology. Also, consider attending a DNA genealogy lecture at the next genealogy conference you attend.

- **Organizing Research Materials – Digital**: Map out a file naming convention and also rename folders if necessary. In addition, don't forget to have at least two forms of file backup! Most genealogists use a cloud platform such as

Dropbox paired with an external hard drive or an automated backup site.

Month 10 To Do List – Review or "Go-Over" Participants

- **Currently Familiar with DNA Genealogy**: If you have already completed one or more DNA test, make sure you are using all the possible tools at your disposal for interpreting results and connecting with others.

- **Organizing Research Materials – Digital**: If you have not set aside your original research files and are still working with them, you will likely have the most work to do in terms of getting organized. Decide on a file naming convention and start using folders to group and sort items.

Genealogy Do-Over – Month 11

Month 11 Topics

- Reviewing Social Media Options
- Building a Research Network
- Reviewing Research Travel Options

Reviewing Social Media Options

Recently I had a conversation with a group of genealogists, of varying ages and levels of experience. One person made the following statement: *You really can't succeed with your genealogy research these days without some use of social media.*

And the reaction? Most of the heads nodded yes. I think that five years ago such a statement would have caused quite a debate. But in the past five years we've seen social media platforms such as Facebook, Twitter and Pinterest take over for the tools we may have used 10 or 20 years ago: queries posted in newsletters, lookup requests posted in online groups or online bulletin boards (remember those?), and even items posted in periodicals like *Everton's Genealogical Helper*.

Social Media Resources

Here are some social media resources that you may not have considered as a way to assist in your genealogical research:

- **Genealogy on Facebook List**
  (http://socialmediagenealogy.com/genealogy-on-facebook-list/) – an amazing resource of 4,500+ links to various pages and groups on Facebook covering almost every aspect of genealogy and family history.

- **Technology for Genealogy**
  (http://www.facebook.com/groups/techgen/) – do you have a technical question related to genealogy software or even what type of scanner to buy? Here is a group of over 18,000 helpful genealogists who will gladly answer any type of question.

- **The Organized Genealogist**
  (https://www.facebook.com/groups/organizedgenealogist/) – over 26,000 people sharing ideas about getting their genealogy materials and digital files organized. Covers filing systems, file naming conventions, archival practices and more. Again, another group where you post a question and other helpful genealogists provide answers and options.

- **Genealogy – Cite Your Sources**
  (http://www.facebook.com/groups/Citesources/) – do have a question about the proper way to cite a specific record? Not sure how to get started on citing your sources? This group will point you in the right direction and show you how easy it is to get your sources cited.

- **Pinterest** – while some people think Pinterest is purely a bunch of BSOs ("bright and shiny objects"), others have been able to build research toolboxes and even ancestor timelines to share with others. Keep in mind that Pinterest is currently the #3 source for website traffic (after Google and Facebook). See the GeneaBloggers boards on Pinterest (http://www.pinterest.com/geneabloggers/) for examples.

- **Twitter** – did you know you can search Twitter without having a Twitter account? Use this link to search the #genealogy "hashtag"
  (http://twitter.com/hashtag/genealogy?f=realtime).
  Remember that a hashtag is simply a label or a way to tell people what the posted message is about.

Review your options and don't be afraid to sign up for a social media account, even if you have to delete it later.

Building a Research Network

You might be wondering, "What does *research network* mean?" Well, by participating in The Genealogy Do-Over, you're already part of a network.

"No genealogist is an island." While pursuing one's roots may seem like a solitary obsession, the truth is that as researchers we soon realize that we cannot "go it alone." Whether it is joining a local genealogical society or engaging with a regular group of researchers at a local library or even joining a genealogy-focused Facebook group, you'll get more out of the entire experience if you slowly build a network

Research Network = Research Toolbox

Don't forget that one of the earlier topics for The Genealogy Do-Over was Building a Research Toolbox. Well, approach building your genealogy network the same way.

This does not mean that you only engage with other genealogists who can offer you some knowledge or help you with your research. It is a two way street. In fact, my approach has been more of a one way street: give your knowledge freely and you will attract others who can help you in the future.

If you have a hard time remembering a person's name, face and genealogy focus area, consider using a contact program or even **Evernote** (http://www.evernote.com) to "keep tabs" on your network. Another great platform, believe it or not, is **LinkedIn** (http://www.linkedin.com). With LinkedIn, you can create your own profile and then seek out other genealogists and people with similar interests. Check out my profile at http://linkedin.com/in/thomasmacentee to see how you can add skills, publications and even articles and then make connections with other users.

Reviewing Research Travel Options

While I travel quite a bit delivering genealogy lectures, I always try to squeeze in some research during a trip. It could be a visit to a local genealogy society library, a cemetery or a historical site. And if I get a chance to take a personal vacation, chances are it will involve genealogy research!

Sponsored Research Trips, Genealogy Cruises and More

While you may have been doing genealogy for years, you may not realize that organized genealogy research trips sponsored by genealogical societies as well as individuals have become very popular. In addition, a genealogy cruise is a great way to take a vacation yet still get a solid genealogy education.

- **Genealogy Society Trips**. Most organized research trips don't include the actual travel expense of arriving at the destination – that is your responsibility. But once there, your accommodations and some meals are covered as well as consultation sessions with professional genealogists. Check out the upcoming trips at the **National Genealogical Society** (http://www.ngsgenealogy.org/cs/research_trips). In addition, **American Ancestors** (aka New England Historic Genealogical Society) offers organized research programs (http://www.americanancestors.org/education/research-tours-and-programs/).

- **Individual or Vendor-Sponsored Trips**. Very often a professional genealogist will organize a research trip to a well-known repository such as the Family History Library in Salt Lake City, Utah or the New York State Library in Albany, New York. Leland Meitzler, of Family Roots Publishing, sponsors the **Salt Lake Christmas Tour** the second week of December each year (https://sites.google.com/site/saltlakechristmastour/) which includes accommodations at the Salt Lake Plaza Hotel right next to the Family History Library, help from consultants and also close to 30 classes throughout the week!

- **Individually-Tailored Trips**. There are times when you know where you want to go and what records you want to look at, but the language and culture might be a barrier. Kathy Wurth of **Family Tree Tours** (http://familytreetours.com/) can assist you with genealogy research in Germany and arranging assistance from local German genealogists who know the records.

- **Genealogy Cruises**. Once you've taken a genealogy cruise, you'll wish that all your genealogy trips were this much fun! Check out the many different cruises offered by **Unlock the Past** (http://www.unlockthepastcruises.com/).

Do-It-Yourself Research Trips

You may prefer to "fly solo" or find that an organized trip does not exist for your specific area of research. Or you may want to attend a national genealogy conference for the first time and then tack on a few days for research. No matter the reason, many genealogists prefer to plan out their own trips.

Here are some areas to review and consider when planning the ultimate genealogy research trip:

- **What Type of Traveler Are You?** This may seem silly, but it really does matter that you understand your travel habits. Why? Well, one reason is that recognizing your "must haves" and how you respond to unexpected changes can help you plan a more productive and enjoyable trip.

- **Preparation and Packing.** Some of us pack at the last minute while others pull out the suitcase weeks ahead of a trip. Whatever works for you, make sure you have a checklist and consider the tools you'll need to get the most out of your research.

- **Preferred Mode of Transportation.** Do you hate to fly? Do you love the nostalgia of a train ride? Or are you a road warrior with an RV ready to go? Use the method of getting there and back that works for you!

- **Accommodations**. Spartan, since you'll spend little time in the room? Or luxurious so you can be pampered after a tough day of research? Where you stay can really set the mood for your entire trip.

- **Expenses**. Create a budget and prioritize items as "must haves" and "optional." Find ways to save money so you can purchase books and souvenirs or splurge on a celebratory dinner the last night of your trip.

- **Emergencies and Last Minute Changes**. Things happen, and how you react and can adapt to change can sink or save a research trip. Make sure you have emergency information for each location including hospitals, urgent care centers and pharmacies. Also let your friends and family know where you are and how to reach you during the trip.

Also, if you plan on traveling with another researcher, make sure you review all the items above with that person. There is nothing worse than being on a trip you have planned all year for, only to find out that you have different "must haves" and "likes" than your traveling companion.

Month 11 To Do List – Full Do-Over Participants

- **Social Media**: If you have not used social media in any form, you may want to go slow and start with one platform, such as Facebook. Also, get help from someone who knows Facebook and can help you get set up. And my best advice: only use it for genealogy. No games, no drama, no nonsense. I've found that with a very narrow use of Facebook (mainly connecting with other genealogists), I've had a much better experience on the site.

- **Research Trip**: If you have not taken a research trip in a while, make sure that you are using your best research (meaning from The Genealogy Do-Over) when you head out. Also, check out all the new apps and sites that make traveling easier!

Month 11 To Do List – Review or "Go-Over" Participants

- **Social Media**: If you are currently using social media, challenge yourself to look at other platforms besides the ones you are currently using.

- **Research Trip**: Although you are "reviewing" your previous genealogy research, there should be no need to retrace your steps and revisit old research locations . . . unless you believe you will locate new items and make progress. Consider trying a sponsored research trip or heading out to a new locale!

Genealogy Do-Over – Month 12

Month 12 Topics

- Sharing research
- Securing research data

Sharing Research

Sharing your genealogy research with others should be a "no-brainer," right? But if you have been doing genealogy for a number of years, you know that it is not always as easy as it should be.

The Do's and Don'ts of Collaborating and Sharing

Here are some ways you can not only benefit from collaborating and sharing with other genealogists, but also repay those researchers who provided valuable information for your own search.

- **Be nice**. The world is a small town. The genealogy community is really a small place and you realize that more and more with the advent of social media. Rude genealogists are duly noted and their reputation will precede them. Kindness offered to others is often returned ten-fold.

- **Ask for attribution and give attribution**. If you want your work to be credited, make sure you are walking the walk on attribution. Drafting the text, sending it to the researcher, and getting their approval is a nice gesture. Also don't be afraid to set some reasonable rules when providing your research and always ask for attribution. Again, providing the ready-made text that credits your work not only makes it easier, but can also help educate the other researcher if they are a newbie.

- **Don't give to get**. It can be difficult to embrace an abundance model, but once you start to share with others, you get the hang of how it works. Don't fall into the "tit for tat" game, but don't be a sucker either.

- **Track your work**. Use **Google Alerts** (http://www.google.com/alerts) to track your copyrighted content. One trick: create a unique phrase for each document or intentionally misspell a word in a phrase and use them as your search string.

You think it would be simple to collaborate and share especially since the genealogy community is generally known as a dedicated and intelligent group of researchers all focused on a similar goal: finding our ancestors. Yet researchers are people, and as such, little things, like the ego and even misinformation or lack of knowledge, can be like sand in the gears of the genealogy machine.

Securing Research Data

Whether you are brand new to genealogy and The Genealogy Do-Over is your first serious effort at research OR you have accumulated years and years of research, let me ask you this question: *What have you done to preserve and "future proof" all your hard work?*

More difficult questions include:

- If you lost all your data, would you be able to recreate it?

- Would you even know where to begin?

- If you died today, do you know what your family would do with your research?

- Have you made plans to preserve your research for generations to come?

Backing Up Your Genealogy Data

Your genealogy research data is an investment reflecting the time and effort you've spent tracing your roots. Like any other investment, your genealogy data should be safe and secure for future use.

The best way to get started on backing up your genealogy data:

- **Create a backup plan**. Just like a research plan for your genealogy, you need to determine what data needs to be backed up and how.

- **Identify data for backup**. Don't forget that as genealogists we tend to store data in many different places. Do you have emails and Internet favorites related to genealogy? Are you certain that information is backed up?

- **Identify a backup method that works for you**. Don't select a backup method, such as copying data each week to a flash drive, if you aren't going to perform the task on a set schedule. Look for automated backups such as cloud backup or an external hard drive with auto-backup software.

- **Test your backup data**. Why bother backing up data if you can't prove it works? Run a test restore on data and make sure you're covered.

- **Future-proof your technology**. Don't rely on outdated tech such as backing up to CDs and DVDs (did you know the coating degrades on these items after just five years?). Upgrade to current technology that has been proven and tested, not the "latest" new thing just on the market.

Future Proofing Your Genealogy Research

Do you have concerns about what will happen to your research once you've passed on? More and more genealogists are realizing that they have not put safeguards into place to ensure that their years of work won't simply be discarded by family members and friends.

Here are areas that require your attention:

- **Take inventory**. Determine what you have and this includes hard copy as well as digital assets and online sites.

- **Include in estate planning**. Create a codicil to your will or make sure there are instructions concerning your genealogy research.

- **Have that conversation with family**. Be very clear about where your genealogy research is located, why it is important, and what you want done with it.

- **Contact organizations**. Determine which libraries, societies and archives will accept all or part of your collection. Donate items you don't need NOW.

- **Post items online**. Consider starting a blog, even a private one, to preserve your family stories. Do the same with a family tree on Ancestry or one of the popular genealogy sites.

- **Do stuff NOW**. Tell your own stories NOW. Write that genealogy book NOW. Interview family members NOW.

I will admit that none of this is easy to do. It is easy to talk about and give advice on the topic, but many of us just tend to put it off . . . until it is too late.

Month 12 To Do List – Full Do-Over Participants

- **Sharing Research**: If you have any trees or items you have shared prior to embarking on The Genealogy Do-Over, consider "warning" others about the presence of any unsourced information. Realize that you are not calling out your mistakes . . . you could even give a nice plug for The Genealogy Do-Over in your explanation!

- **Securing research data**: Seriously consider creating an action plan for both backing up your genealogy research data <u>and</u> ensuring that it is preserved for future generations.

Month 12 To Do List – Review or "Go-Over" Participants

- **Sharing Research**: If you have the time (and the energy) and you are correcting your research, consider doing the same for any online trees or messages or other information you've shared with others.

- **Securing research data**: Seriously consider creating an action plan for both backing up your genealogy research data <u>and</u> ensuring that it is preserved for future generations.

Reviewing the Journey

Wow . . . 12 months and didn't it just seem to zoom by? I can't speak for those who participated in The Genealogy Do-Over. I can, however, relate what I've learned and discovered during a year of The Genealogy Do-Over:

- **There is a need for change**: Those who have been doing genealogy for years and years have begun to realize that their early genealogy research may not provide the foundation that they want for a solid family tree.

- **No guilt, no shame, and no regrets**: More importantly, there has been an honest discussion about our past practices and ways to improve them. With the input of thousands of participants, we created a "safe space" where anyone can admit they were a name collector or didn't cite their sources.

- **Collaboration counts**: Genealogists have always been collaborators; this is nothing new. In years past we would gather at society meetings and exchange information as well as research tips. We would attend conferences to improve our research knowledge and to network with others. Now with social media and groups such as The Genealogy Do-Over Facebook Group, the collaborative tradition continues. Remember this: very few of our ancestors arrived in a new place and could have survived on their own. They counted on the wisdom and knowledge of those that arrived before them.

- **Honor and respect**: I've also learned that genealogists are people (amazing, right?) We all have our quirks, our biases . . . we are human after all. Even with over 10,000 members in the Facebook Group, we've managed to agree on many issues and yet disagree on how to approach them. Many people told me I was crazy to try and "supervise the sand box" and that doing so would just suck the life and energy out of me. It turned out that the opposite has been true: I've enjoyed the dialog and I've gained real insights as to what drives and motivates genealogists. There have been less than five times when I've had to delete a post or ban a member of the group for various reasons such as being rude or hijacking posts. I think this track record says quite a bit about the genealogy community.

- **A big thank you to the professionals**: One of the most amazing aspects of The Genealogy Do-Over is how the concept has been embraced by various professional genealogists. And I don't mean that they've "capitalized" on an active audience or tried to sell their own products and services to the crowd. Many of them have spent hours posting advice in the Facebook Group on citing sources, locating records, tracking research and more. In particular, Elizabeth Shown Mills has been a regular presence and I'm grateful for all her contributions.

- **Genealogy was meant to be fun**: Have I had fun during The Genealogy Do-Over? I have and it has been due to the combination of energy and humor contributed by group members. Thanks to everyone who posted a funny cartoon or quotation. Thanks to those who were able to tell their funny and even most embarrassing stories about their early research. If genealogy isn't fun, I just don't think I would be doing it.

- **A continual journey:** And finally, I've come to realize that you just can't do The Genealogy Do-Over in a matter of weeks. No one can, not even me. When I created this program, I wanted something short and sweet and that would serve as a foundation for constant and continued improvement of genealogical research skills. I think that has been accomplished.

Once again, thank you for being a part of this amazing journey. Your participation, your input at the Facebook Group, your comments on live lectures and webinars and more – all of these have energized me and have made me even more committed to continue leading a discussion on improving genealogical research habits.

Going Forward To Do List – Full Do-Over Participants

- Evaluate how The Genealogy Do-Over has improved your research habits. Consider focusing on those topics where you feel you still need improvement.

Going Forward To Do List – Review or "Go-Over" Participants

- Evaluate how The Genealogy Do-Over has improved your research habits even in a "review" perspective of your existing research.

The Genealogy Do-Over for Genealogy Societies

During the course of Cycle 1 of The Genealogy Do-Over in early 2015, it became apparent to many genealogy society leaders and members that The Genealogy Do-Over could be used as a program to educate and motivate society members to improve their genealogical research. As a long-time supporter of genealogy societies, I'm all in favor of any program that can be developed to carry forward the message of The Genealogy Do-Over.

Here are some suggestions on how to implement The Genealogy Do-Over with your society:

- Create a Special Interest Group (SIG) focused on The Genealogy Do-Over. Most SIGs meet monthly which is the perfect format for tackling each set of topics.

- Use excerpts from The Genealogy Do-Over Workbook in your society's newsletter as "lessons" for your membership.

A Note on Copyright and Attribution

While my overall goal with The Genealogy Do-Over is to encourage participation by as many genealogists as possible, I still need to protect my work product and intellectual property developed as part of this effort.

To that end, if your genealogy society would like to reprint portions of this workbook in a newsletter or quarterly, please use the following "byline" at the end of each article excerpted:

Resources

General

Dropbox
http://www.dropbox.com

Evernote
http://www.evernote.com

Evidence Explained
http://www.evidenceexplained.com

Genealogy Do-Over Mailing List
http://www.geneabloggers.com/gendo-over-emails

Google Alerts
http://www.google.com/alerts

LinkedIn
http://www.linkedin.com

Skype
http://www.skype.com

DNA Research

DNAeXplained – Genetic Genealogy
http://dna-explained.com/

GedMatch
http://v2.gedmatch.com/

ISOGG Wiki
http://www.isogg.org/wiki/Wiki_Welcome_Page

Jump into Genetic Genealogy: Use Genealogical DNA Testing to Solve Family Mysteries
http://ftu.familytreemagazine.com/jump-into-genetic-genealogy-use-genealogical-dna-testing-to-solve-family-mysteries/

Kitty Cooper's Blog
http://blog.kittycooper.com/

The Genetic Genealogist
http://www.thegeneticgenealogist.com/

The Legal Genealogists – DNA
http://www.legalgenealogist.com/blog/category/dna/

Your Genetic Genealogist
http://www.yourgeneticgenealogist.com/

Facebook Groups

The Genealogy Do-Over
https://www.facebook.com/groups/genealogydoover/

Genealogy – Cite Your Sources
http://www.facebook.com/groups/Citesources/

Technology for Genealogy
http://www.facebook.com/groups/techgen/

The Organized Genealogist
http://www.facebook.com/groups/organizedgenealogist/

Getting Organized

The Organized Genealogist
http://www.theorganizedgenealogist.net/.

Organize Your Family History
http://organizeyourfamilyhistory.com/

Cyndi's List – Organizing
http://www.cyndislist.com/organizing/

The Family Curator
http://www.thefamilycurator.com/

Social Media

Genealogy on Facebook List
http://socialmediagenealogy.com/genealogy-on-facebook-list/

Pinterest
http://www.pinterest.com

Pinterest – The Genealogy Do-Over
http://www.pinterest.com/geneabloggers/genealogy-do-overtm/

Pinterest – GeneaBloggers
http://www.pinterest.com/geneabloggers/

Twitter
http://www.twitter.com

Twitter – Search Genealogy
http://twitter.com/hashtag/genealogy?f=realtime

Videos

The Genealogy Do-Over Channel – YouTube
http://www.geneabloggers.com/gdovideos

Tools and Templates

Excel Version – Genealogy Research Log
http://www.geneabloggers.com/genreslog

About The Author

Photo by Dena Palamedes

What happens when a "tech guy" with a love for history gets laid off during The Great Recession of 2008? You get Thomas MacEntee, a genealogy professional based in the United States who is also a blogger, educator, author, social media connector, online community builder and more.

Thomas was laid off after a 25-year career in the information technology field, so he started his own genealogy-related business called High Definition Genealogy. He also created an online community of over 3,000 family history bloggers known as GeneaBloggers. His most recent endeavor, Hack Genealogy, is an attempt to "re-purpose today's technology for tomorrow's genealogy."

Thomas describes himself as a lifelong learner with a background in a multitude of topics who has finally figured out what he does best: teach, inspire, instigate, and serve as a curator and go-to-guy for concept nurturing and inspiration. Thomas is a big believer in success, and that we all succeed when we help each other find success.

Check out Thomas' author page at http://geneaguides.com

Made in the USA
San Bernardino, CA
29 December 2016